GEOGRAPHY FACT FILES

MOUNTAINS

Anna Claybourne

A⁺
Smart Apple Media

GEOGRAPHY FACT FILES

First published in 2004 by Hodder Wayland

338 Euston Road, London NW1 3BH, United Kingdom

Hodder Wayland is an imprint of Hodder Children's Books, a division of Hodder Headline Limited. This edition published under license from Hodder Children's Books. All rights reserved.

Produced for Hodder Wayland by

Monkey Puzzle Media Ltd

Gissing's Farm, Fressingfield, Suffolk IP21 5SH

United Kingdom

Copyright © 2004 Hodder Wayland

Editor	Catherine Burch
Designer	Jamie Asher
Picture Researcher	Sally Cole
Illustrator	Michael Posen
Consultant	Michael Allaby

Published in the United States by Smart Apple Media

2140 Howard Drive West

North Mankato, Minnesota 56003

U.S. publication copyright © 2005 Smart Apple Media International copyright reserved in all countries. No part of this book may be reproduced in any form without written permission from the publisher.

Printed in China

Library of Congress Cataloging-in-Publication Data

Claybourne, Anna.

Mountains / by Anna Claybourne.

p. cm. — (Geography fact files)

Includes bibliographical references and index.

ISBN 1-58340-426-0

1. Mountains—Juvenile literature. 2. Mountain ecology—Juvenile literature. [1. Mountains. 2. Mountain ecology. 3. Ecology.] I. Title. II. Series.

GB512.C55 2004

551.43'2—dc22   2003067396

9 8 7 6 5 4 3 2 1

Acknowledgements

We are grateful to the following for permission to reproduce photographs: Alamy 19 bottom, 47; Corbis 1 (Galen Rowell), 6 (Bettmann), 9 top (Danny Lehman), 15, 17 (Galen Rowell), 27 (James A Sugar), 28 (Gunther Marx Photography), 39 bottom (Marc Muench), 40 (Dewitt Jones); Corbis Digital Stock 3 bottom inset, 33; FLPA 14 (Steve McCutcheon), 45 (David Hosking); Getty Images front cover (William Smithey Jr.); James Davis Travel Photography 5 top, 11 top, 32, 46; Mountain Camera 19 top; Nature Picture Library 22 (Konstantin Mikhailov), 25 top (Juan Manuel Borrero); NHPA 29 (T Kitchin and V Hurst); PA Photos 26 (Alison Hargreaves), 31 top (EPA); Rex Features 9 bottom (SIPA), 36 (B Veysett/SIPA), 41 (Lehtikuva Oy), 43 top (SIPA); Robert Harding Picture Library 3 middle inset (Tony Demin/International Stock), 4 (S Sassoon), 12 (Tony Waltham), 20 (Ron Sanford/International Stock), 25 bottom (Tony Waltham), 37 (E Simaner), 39 top (Tony Demin/International Stock); Still Pictures 3 top inset (Peter Weimann), 5 bottom (Roland Seitre), 11 bottom (Alain Compost), 21 top (Peter Weimann), 21 bottom (Fritz Polking), 30 (Hartmut Schwarzbach), 31 bottom (Edward Parker), 34 (John Isaac), 35 top (Adrian Arbib), 35 bottom (Mark Edwards), 38 (Chiaus Lotcher), 42 (Daniel Dancer), 43 bottom (Fritz Polking); Swift Imagery 10 (David Young), 13 (G R Park), 44.

Title page picture: K2, now officially measured to be the world's second-highest mountain.

CONTENTS

WHAT IS A MOUNTAIN?

Everyone knows what a mountain looks like—and yet there is no absolute definition of what a mountain really is. Most geographers (people who study Earth) agree that a mountain is a big piece of land, with steep, sloping sides, that sticks up from the land around it. Some say that to be a true mountain, it has to be more than 3,280 feet (1,000 m) high (measured from sea level). Others believe that any large, steep-sided lump of land can be called a mountain.

LOCATION FILE

HOME OF THE GODS
The ancient Greeks believed that their gods lived at the top of Mount Olympus, a 9,568-foot-high (2,917 m) mountain in northern Greece. Many mountains around the world are regarded as sacred, including Mount Fuji in Japan and Mount Kenya in Kenya, Africa.

MOUNTAIN RANGES
Because of the way they are formed (see page 8), most mountains are found in mountain ranges. These are long groups, or chains, of mountains that can stretch for hundreds or even thousands of miles. For example, the Andes mountain range reaches all the way down the western side of South America, from Colombia in the north to Patagonia (the southern part of Chile and Argentina) in the south.

Rising 19,335 feet (5,895 m) into the air, Kilimanjaro, in Tanzania, East Africa, has been regarded as sacred by local people for centuries. Early explorers also thought it was magical because it had snow on top, despite being almost on the equator.

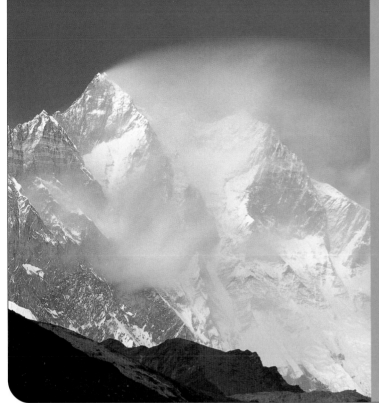

Mount Everest is the highest mountain in the world.

FACT FILE

TOP FIVE MOUNTAINS

This is a list of the five highest mountains in the world. Mountain heights can change (see pages 10 and 11), and they can be measured in different ways, so height lists may vary from book to book.

Mountain	Location	Height
Everest	China/Nepal	29,028 feet (8,850 m)
K2	China/Pakistan	28,244 feet (8,611 m)
Kanchenjunga	India/Nepal	28,198 feet (8,597 m)
Lhotse	China/Nepal	27,932 feet (8,516 m)
Makalu	China/Nepal	27,818 feet (8,481 m)

A DIFFERENT WORLD

Mountains have their own climate. They are colder and windier than the low-lying lands around them, and the air contains less oxygen. Because the weather, landscape, and conditions on a mountain are different, the wildlife is different, too. Above a certain height, it's too cold for trees to grow, and smaller plants have to be tough to survive. Mountain animals also have to **adapt** to living in these difficult conditions. They may have extra-thick hair or fur for keeping warm, or extra-large feet so they don't sink into the deep snow.

LIVING IN THE MOUNTAINS

Because of their rough **terrain** and harsh climate, most mountain areas are undeveloped. They have few roads, towns, or cities and are mostly wilderness. However, people do live in the mountains, usually in small villages. They herd mountain animals, grow high-**altitude** crops, or work as guides for mountain tourists.

A woman in Bhutan, high in the mountains, weaving yak wool.

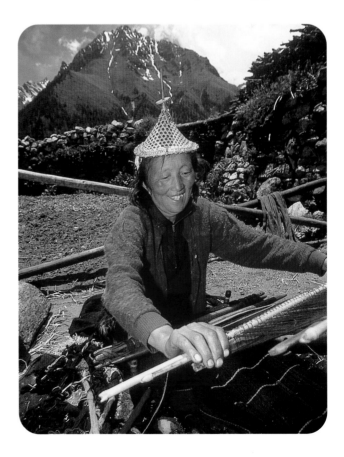

WHERE ARE MOUNTAINS?

Mountains are found all over the planet. There are big mountain ranges on every continent, and most countries contain mountains of some kind. Altogether, mountainous regions make up 20 percent of the world's total land area. There are also many more mountains under the sea.

THE BIGGEST MOUNTAINS

The highest mountains in the world, including Mount Everest, the tallest of all, are in the Himalayan mountain range. The Himalayas lie in the middle of Asia, overlapping India, China, Pakistan, and the tiny kingdoms of Nepal and Bhutan. Other massive mountain ranges include the Andes, the Alps, the Rockies, the Urals, and the Atlas Mountains.

PEOPLE FILE

HANNIBAL

Hannibal is famous for crossing the Alps with a team of elephants. He was a general from Carthage, in North Africa, which was at war with the Roman Empire in the third century B.C. In 218 B.C., Hannibal planned an attack on Rome from Spain. He chose the difficult route over the Alps—and took the elephants—in order to take the Romans by surprise. It took his army 15 days to cross the mountains, and many of his elephants died on the way.

A painting of Hannibal and his army crossing an Alpine mountain pass.

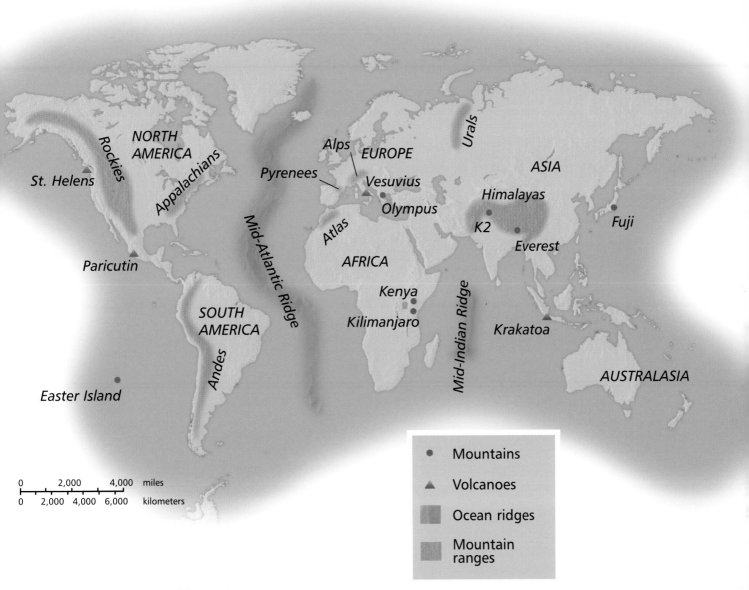

This map shows the world's main mountain ranges and a selection of individual mountain peaks.

MOUNTAINS UNDER THE SEA

Mountains that rise from the seabed are sometimes called **seamounts**. Like mountains on land, they can occur in ranges or on their own. One of the biggest undersea mountain ranges is the Mid-Atlantic Ridge, which runs down the middle of the Atlantic Ocean. Sometimes, the peaks of undersea mountains stick out of the sea and form islands. The islands of Iceland, Ascension, and the Azores are all parts of the Mid-Atlantic Ridge that rise above sea level.

LOCATION FILE

EASTER ISLAND

Easter Island is a tiny island in the Pacific Ocean, more than 1,240 miles (2,000 km) from the nearest land. Although the island itself is small, it's just the tip of a giant volcano that rises nearly 9,840 feet (3,000 m) from the seabed. The volcano has not erupted since people settled on the island around 1,500 years ago.

MAKING MOUNTAINS

Mountains are made when part of the hard, rocky crust that covers the earth moves upward. This can happen in various ways. Most types of mountains— fold, fault, dome, and volcanic—get their names from the ways in which they were formed. The formation of mountains is called orogenesis.

FOLD MOUNTAINS

Earth's outer crust is made up of huge sections called **tectonic plates**, fitted together like a jigsaw. They move very slowly, floating on the **magma** that's inside Earth. Sometimes the plates push against each other, and their edges are slowly forced up into massive folds and wrinkles—or mountains. Most of Earth's large mountain ranges, including the Himalayas, the Andes, the Alps, and the Rockies, were formed in this way.

FAULT-BLOCK MOUNTAINS

Fault-block mountains are made when a huge block of rock separates from the rest of Earth's crust, and is pushed upward or sinks downward.

BULGING DOMES

Dome mountains are a type of mountain made when magma—the hot molten rock under Earth's crust—pushes upward into softer overlying rocks, then cools and hardens. The weather then wears away the softer material. The Adirondacks, in New York, and the mountains of the Lake District in England formed in this way and were worn away by **glaciers** during the last ice age.

Fold mountains form when Earth's crust folds, or buckles, under pressure from two land masses pushing together.

Fold

Fault-block mountains form when a section of Earth's crust separates from the crust around it, and rises or sinks.

Fault

Fault

VOLCANIC ERUPTIONS

Fold mountains and fault-block mountains take millions of years to form, but a volcano can grow quickly—sometimes in just a few weeks. Volcanoes happen when magma from inside the earth erupts (bursts) through the crust, cools, and hardens into rock. Volcanoes are common at places where tectonic plates meet. For example, there are a lot of volcanoes in the Andes mountain range, where one plate pushes underneath another. Volcanoes can also form individually in areas where Earth's crust is weak and magma can push through. Find out more about volcanoes on pages 12 and 13.

Find out more about volcanoes on pages 12 and 13.

LOCATION FILE

THE FOLDED HIMALAYAS

The Himalayas are a classic example of fold mountains. They first started to grow about 50 million years ago, when the plate carrying India pushed against the rest of Asia. The two land masses squeezed together and crumpled up into a massive mountain range.

LOCATION FILE

BIRTH OF A VOLCANO

In 1943, a Mexican farmer named Dominic Pulido noticed a strange crack in one of his cornfields. Hot ash and lava started to come out of it, forming a cone shape. Within two months the new volcano, named Paricutin, was more than 984 feet (300 m) high. Today, Paricutin (below), which has stopped erupting, is a 1,391-foot-high (424 m) cone covering an area of more than 10 square miles (25 sq km).

The sharp peaks of the Himalayas (below) were made by the folding of Earth's crust.

HOW MOUNTAINS CHANGE

They might look solid and permanent, but mountains are changing all the time—even those that formed many millions of years ago. While Earth's plates keep pushing mountains upward, their peaks change shape as they erode (wear down) over time.

PUSHING UP

The tectonic plates that make up Earth's crust are still moving very slowly—about as fast as a person's fingernails grow. That means that as the plates push together, some mountain ranges, such as the Himalayas and the Alps, are still growing. Mount Everest, for example, increases in height by at least .4 inches (1 cm) every year.

The Matterhorn, in the Swiss Alps, is famous for its unusual shape. The Alps formed as fold mountains when Italy and Europe pushed together. Glaciers then carved away the sides of the Matterhorn, giving it its "horn" shape.

WEARING DOWN

Erosion happens when wind, rain, and other forces wear rock and soil away. Because of their cold, harsh weather and steep, exposed slopes, mountains erode faster than the land around them. Gradually, a typical fold mountain wears down from a pointed peak into a smooth, rounded bump. The eroded material falls down into valleys, and rivers wash it away toward the sea to become, finally, part of the seabed. Over millions of years, rocks that make up Earth's crust move around in a cycle, being constantly pushed up and then eroded away. Geologists (scientists who study rocks and **landforms**) call this cycle the erosion cycle.

FACT FILE

WHAT CAUSES EROSION?

Here are some of the things that can cause erosion on mountains:

- Wind blows soil and small rocks away.
- Rain washes soil down steep slopes.
- Ice expands as it freezes, cracking rocks into smaller pieces that can then be blown or washed away. Glaciers—huge, moving rivers of ice—carve valleys in mountainsides.
- Animals wear down tracks and dig burrows, dislodging rocks and soil.
- Humans erode mountains by wearing away paths and scrambling over rocks.

This is Half Dome, in California. Its dome shape was probably made by underground magma pushing up through other rocks. Over time, the surrounding rocks eroded away, and glaciers flowing down the valley scraped away half of the dome.

LOCATION FILE

KRAKATOA

In 1883, Krakatoa, an island volcano in Indonesia, exploded so spectacularly that most of the mountain was blown away. Ash from the eruption landed as far as 3,720 miles (6,000 km) away, and more than 36,000 people were killed—mostly by the **tsunamis** the explosion caused.

SUDDEN CHANGES

Sometimes, erosion eats away at a mountain peak until a huge chunk of rock falls off, giving the mountain a new shape almost overnight. Volcanic mountains can also change shape very suddenly, building up pressure inside until they are blown apart in a massive explosion. This happened to Mount St. Helens, in Washington, in 1980. For several weeks, magma built up inside the mountain, making it bulge on one side. There were several small eruptions and earthquakes. Finally, on May 18, the whole side of the mountain blew off. It was the biggest volcanic eruption in American history. Fifty-seven people were killed, and a huge area of farmland and forest was destroyed.

Small eruptions like this one still take place at the remains of Krakatoa, in Indonesia.

VOLCANOES

Volcanoes are mountains that are formed when magma from inside Earth bursts, or erupts, through Earth's crust. A volcano can erupt many times. Each time, more magma comes out and builds up around the volcano, making it bigger and bigger.

INSIDE A VOLCANO

Most volcanoes are cone-shaped, because they are formed by rock and ash heaping up around the spot where the magma breaks through Earth's crust. The magma moves up through a channel in the middle of the volcano, known as the vent. Sometimes, smaller channels, called dikes, develop off the main vent. Once magma leaves a vent or a dike and flows out of the volcano, it is known as lava.

ACTIVE, DORMANT, OR EXTINCT?

If a volcano is **active**, it means it erupts regularly. Stromboli, in Italy, and Arenal, in Costa Rica, are examples of active volcanoes that erupt almost every day. A **dormant** volcano, such as Haleakala, in Hawaii, is one that hasn't erupted for a long time but could erupt again. An **extinct** volcano is one that volcanologists (volcano scientists) think will never erupt again.

HOT SPOTS AND THE RING OF FIRE

Volcanoes often occur near the edges of Earth's tectonic plates. This is because Earth's crust is more likely to be cracked there. Most of the world's active volcanoes are found in a ring around the Pacific Ocean, which lies on top of one big plate called the Pacific plate. This ring of volcanic activity is called the "Ring of Fire."

However, volcanoes can occur in the middle of plates, too. They may form where there is an area of extra-hot magma, called a "hot spot," under Earth's crust.

The remains of Mount St. Helens, in Washington, which exploded in a massive volcanic eruption in 1980. Another mountain, Mount Rainier, can be seen in the background.

LOCATION FILE

INNER-CITY VOLCANO

In Edinburgh, Scotland, a castle stands on top of a giant rock in the middle of the city. The rock is actually a volcanic plug—the cooled, hardened vent of an ancient, extinct volcano. After the plug formed, the rest of the mountain was eroded away, leaving a solid rock column.

Edinburgh's Castle Rock, formed from the plug of an extinct volcano.

FACT FILE

FAMOUS VOLCANOES

NAME	PLACE	WHY IS IT FAMOUS?
Vesuvius	Italy	Erupted in A.D. 79, destroying the town of Pompei.
Fuji	Japan	Famous for its beauty, this volcano is regarded as sacred.
Mount St. Helens	U.S.	Blew apart in a massive eruption in 1980.
Mauna Loa	Hawaii	Measured from the seabed, this is the biggest volcano in the world.
Ojos del Salado	Chile	At 22,583 feet (6,885 m), it's the world's highest volcano measured from sea level.

STUDYING MOUNTAINS

Studying mountains involves a lot of guesswork. One can't cut a mountain in half to see how it's made, or go back in time to see when an extinct volcano last erupted. Instead, most mountain scientists think up theories (ideas about how things work) based on looking at mountain shapes and rocks and taking careful measurements.

LOOKING AT SHAPES

Scientists can tell a lot about a mountain from the way it looks. If it's smooth, rounded, and worn away, it's probably very old, while mountains that formed more recently are sharp and jagged (see page 10). Other shapes can hold clues about different types of erosion. For example, long, deep, U-shaped mountain valleys were formed by glaciers—rivers of ice that move slowly down a mountain, pushing rock and soil out of the way. If a mountain has glacial valleys, it means that it was shaped during one of Earth's ice ages, when the weather was much colder and icier than it is now.

These rocks in Yukon, Canada, are made up of dozens of rock layers, or strata. When the layers formed, they were horizontal, but movements in Earth's crust have tilted and pushed them up.

LAYERS OF ROCK

Much of Earth's rock is made up of layers called **strata**. They were formed long ago when layers of mud or sand settled onto the land or seabed. Over time, they were compressed (squashed) into different types of hard rock. In places where Earth's crust has been pushed up into mountains, rock strata can act as a record of the past. Patterns in the strata show how rock has moved, broken, or folded, while fossils trapped in the layers can reveal when the rocks were formed.

VOLCANO SCIENCE

As well as studying how volcanoes were formed
and how they work, volcanologists try to predict
eruptions. They measure movements in the ground
to see if pressure is building up inside a volcano,
and collect material from active volcanoes' craters.
Poisonous gases, flying rocks, and lava flows
sometimes cost volcanologists their lives. However,
volcanologists also save many thousands of lives by
warning when big eruptions will take place.

MAPPING MOUNTAINS

Mapping means representing real-life landscapes on a flat piece of paper—a map. Mountains are difficult to map for two main reasons. First, they are remote and difficult to travel over, so taking all the right measurements is hard work. Second, they stick up from the ground, so cartographers (map-makers) have to find ways to show them in two dimensions.

HOW HIGH?

The height of a mountain—or any tall object—can be measured using triangulation, a kind of simple math that uses triangles. If the length of one or more sides of a triangle and two of its angles are known, the lengths of the other sides can be figured out. Triangulation has been used for centuries to calculate mountain heights, but it is not always accurate.

Modern triangulation systems use lasers to get very accurate measurements. But different teams still get different results, and people still disagree about the heights of mountains.

Another way to measure altitude (height above sea level) is with a barometer, which measures air pressure. This works because air pressure drops as one moves higher up. But since weather also affects air pressure, barometers are not always accurate.

The diagram below shows how triangulation measurements are taken and calculated.

This angle is calculated using a dangling string to give the vertical

This distance can be measured by shining a laser between the two points

When the other measurements are known, the height of the mountain can be calculated

n°

90°

This distance is measured along the ground

MOUNTAINS ON MAPS

To show hills and mountains on a flat map, cartographers use contour lines. A contour line is a continuous line marking a particular height. For example, a map could have a contour line at every 33 feet (10 m) of altitude. The closer the lines are together, the steeper the real-life slope is.

SATELLITES AND COMPUTERS

Today, many maps are made using **remote sensing**, which uses **satellites** orbiting Earth to photograph and measure landscapes. On the ground, **GPS (Global Positioning System)** equipment exchanges signals with satellites, allowing people to figure out exactly where they are. People can also make 3D maps using computerized **GIS (Geographic Information System)** technology. It can display an image of a mountainous landscape that can be viewed from any angle.

A mountaineer with his tent and sleeping bag halfway up K2, now officially measured to be the world's second-highest mountain.

LOCATION FILE

CONFUSING K2

K2, in the Himalayas, is the second-highest mountain in the world, but at one point it was thought to be the highest. In 1987, a British team measured the mountain and got a result of 29,031 feet (8,851 m)—higher than Mount Everest. Debate raged until new measurements were taken in 1996. K2's official height is now 28,244 feet (8,611 m).

MOUNTAIN ZONES

A big mountain can contain many different landscapes and climates. Near the bottom, the surroundings are similar to a lowland area, with forests (except in polar regions) and gentle slopes. As one climbs higher, and the weather gets colder, the trees give way to meadows, steep rocky slopes, and, finally, snow and ice. Because of this, geographers divide mountains into several different levels, or zones, each with its own landscape and vegetation (plant life).

TROPICAL OR TEMPERATE?

Although most big mountains have zones, the zones are different in different parts of the world. In hot, tropical places near the equator, mountains have hot, wet rainforests or hot, dry grasslands near the bottom, with bamboo, flowering plants, and moors higher up. Mountains in cooler temperate regions, such as the Alps, have **deciduous** forests lower down, **evergreen** forests higher up, and rocky meadows near the top.

THE TREELINE

On big mountains, there is usually a line known as the treeline, above which very few trees can grow. This is partly because it's too cold and windy for them. It's also because not much soil can cling to the steep, rocky slopes high up a mountain, so there's nothing for tree roots to hold on to.

This diagram shows the zones of a mountain—on the left, as in a tropical region, and on the right, as in a temperate region.

TROPICAL   TEMPERATE

Snowline

Steep rocky slopes

Alpine zone: grass, rocks, and large flowering plants such as giant lobelias

Alpine zone: grassy, rocky meadows with small flowering plants such as buttercups

Treeline

Subalpine zone: moors with occasional trees

Subalpine zone: a few tough evergreen trees

Bamboo zone: bamboo or similar grass-like or shrub-like plants

Coniferous forest zone: thick forests of evergreen trees

Montane forest zone: damp, misty mountain forests

Mixed forest zone: a combination of evergreen and deciduous trees

Rainforest or grassland zone: hot, steamy rainforests or hot, dry grasslands

Deciduous forest zone: deciduous trees

In this photo, the three mountain zones can be seen clearly. The alpine meadow, covered in grass, flowers, and occasional rocks, is in the foreground. Higher up lie the rocky slopes, and above them the icy mountain peak.

SNOW AND ICE

The tops of very high mountains, wherever they are in the world, are permanently covered with snow and ice. The area where it begins is called the snowline. Many mountains, such as those in the Alps, are completely covered by snow in winter.

CHANGING RIVERS

The headwaters, or starting points, of most big rivers are in mountain areas. A river begins as a small, cold, clear mountain stream, tumbling down the rocky mountainside and over waterfalls. As more streams flow into it, the stream gets wider and becomes a river. As the slopes flatten out, the river forms loops and winding curves on its way to the sea.

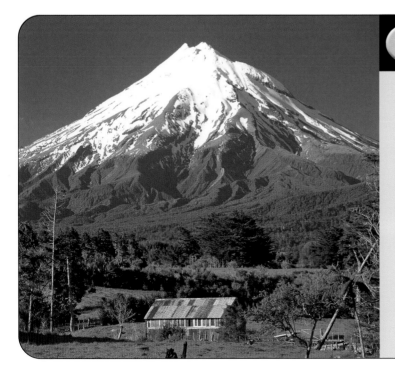

LOCATION FILE

THE ZONES OF MOUNT EGMONT

Mount Egmont (left), also called Mount Taranaki, is a dormant volcano in New Zealand. Its neat cone shape shows off several mountain zones very clearly. This picture shows the mountain in summer. In winter, it is completely covered in snow and ice.

MOUNTAIN WILDLIFE

Like all wildlife, the plants and animals that live on mountains have adapted to their habitats, or surroundings. Because mountain zones create several different mountain habitats, different types of wildlife are found at different levels.

KEEPING WARM

Mountains are cold and windy, and there's not much shelter. To keep warm, many mountain animals have extra-thick hair or fur. Yaks in the Himalayas have two layers of hair: a thick, windproof outer coat, and a soft, fluffy layer underneath. Snow leopards and snowshoe hares have fur not only all over their bodies, but on the soles of their feet, too. Many animals, including wildcats and birds such as snow finches, can fluff up their fur or feathers to trap a layer of warm air around their bodies. Even some mountain plants, such as the alpine silverleaf phacelia, have "fur" to protect them from the cold climate.

FINDING FOOD

Food can be scarce in the mountains, especially in winter, so animals have to be good at finding it. Pikas—small furry animals similar to rabbits— collect grass in the summer, then dry it in the sun and store it to eat in the winter. Lammergeiers (a type of vulture) feed on the bodies of goats and sheep that have died falling from steep rocks. Small birds called wallcreepers have special beaks for picking insects out of cracks between rocks, while Dall sheep can survive on a winter diet of lichen, moss, and frozen grass.

These salmon are leaping up a waterfall in a mountain river in order to make their way back to the mountain stream where they were born. There they will breed, then die.

MOUNTAIN ANIMAL FACTS

To survive in mountain weather and terrain, mountain animals have to be tough. Here are some of their amazing feats:

• Bar-headed geese fly right over the tops of the Himalayas 29,520 feet (9,000 m) up—as high as an airliner.

• Jumping spiders have been found living in the snow 22,960 feet (7,000 m) up on Mount Everest.

• Big rocks and crags don't get in a cougar's way. It can jump more than 16 feet (5 m) straight upward.

• Wild salmon can leap 11 feet (3.5 m) out of the water, allowing them to jump over waterfalls as they swim up mountain streams.

• The mountain iguana can survive with a body temperature of only 35 °F (1.5 °C)—just above freezing.

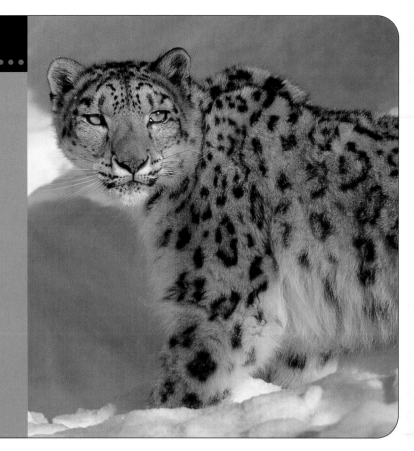

PLANTS ON TOP

Mountain plants such as alpine forget-me-nots and dwarf willows are usually stockier than their cousins in lowland areas, with thicker stems and shorter branches. By clinging close to the ground, they avoid being damaged or blown away by mountain winds.

Above: Snow leopards live in high mountains in Asia, such as the Himalayas.

Below: A Japanese macaque, also known as a snow monkey, warming itself in a natural hot spring.

LOCATION FILE

MONKEY MOUNTAIN

On the slopes of the Shiga Kogen volcano, in Japan, Japanese macaques (a type of monkey) have found a brilliant way to keep warm. They spend their days sitting in hot springs that bubble up between the hot underground volcanic rocks.

MOUNTAIN ECOSYSTEMS

An ecosystem is a habitat and all the plants and animals that live in it together. Plants and animals eat each other and depend on each other to survive, so if one animal disappears from an ecosystem, it affects the others, too. A mountain can be seen as one big ecosystem. Each zone, such as an alpine meadow or a tropical cloudforest, is also its own smaller ecosystem.

FOOD CHAINS AND WEBS

In the wild, animals survive by eating plants or other animals. One species eats another, and in turn is eaten by another, forming a sequence known as a food chain. Plants are always at the bottom of a food chain, with large hunting animals, such as big cats, at the top. A food web is a complicated system containing many interconnected food chains. Each animal in an ecosystem, such as a mountain forest, has its own place, or **niche**, in the food web.

CHANGING SURROUNDINGS

In an ecosystem, living things have to fit in with their surroundings in order to survive. When the weather and seasons change, plants and animals have to change, too. Brown bears, for example, eat different foods in different seasons—such as eggs in the spring, salmon that breed in mountain rivers in the summer, and berries in the fall. Many animals (such as bears and marmots) spend the cold mountain winters hibernating in a cozy den or burrow. Hibernation is a kind of deep winter sleep, during which an animal doesn't need to eat.

West Caucasian turs live in the Caucasus Mountains. In the summer, they feed high up on the mountain slopes. In the winter, they move lower down to nibble the leaves of trees and bushes.

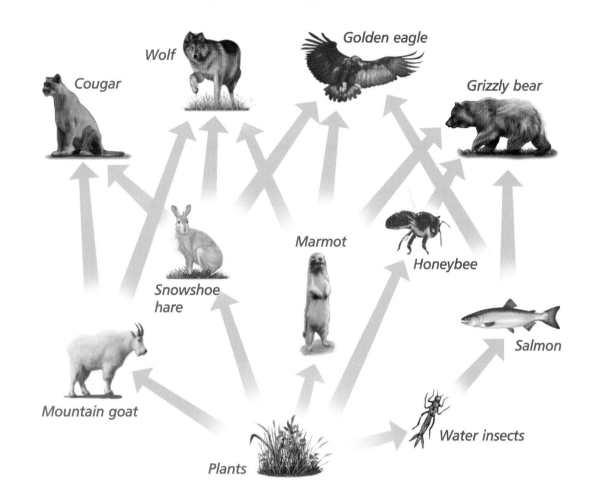

Cougar

Wolf

Golden eagle

Grizzly bear

Snowshoe hare

Marmot

Honeybee

Salmon

Mountain goat

Plants

Water insects

This diagram shows a simplified version of a food web in a North American mountain forest. Each arrow points from something that is eaten to an animal that eats it.

LIVING TOGETHER

While some living things in an ecosystem feed on each other, some help each other to survive. This kind of teamwork between two living things is called **symbiosis.** Lichens, which cling to high mountain rocks where few plants can survive, are actually made up of two living things, a fungus and an alga, in symbiosis. The fungus, a type of living thing similar to a mushroom, surrounds the alga, protecting it, and keeping it damp. Meanwhile, the alga, a type of tiny plant, uses sunlight to make food for both itself and the fungus.

FACT FILE

FOOD WEB LEVELS
Ecologists (scientists who study ecosystems) divide living things into different types, depending on their position in the food web.

• CONSUMERS "Consumers" is another word for "eaters." Animals that eat plants are called primary consumers. Animals that eat other animals are called secondary consumers.
• PRODUCERS Plants are called producers because they make (or produce) food using sunlight.
• DECOMPOSERS These include mushrooms and bacteria. They feed on dead plants and animals and help them to decompose (rot) and break down into chemicals that end up in the soil. This makes food for plants, and so the cycle begins again.

MOUNTAIN WEATHER

Mountains have very extreme weather: gale-force winds, freezing temperatures, and a lot of rain and snow. This is partly because the shape of a mountain changes the weather around it, creating its own local climate.

THE HIGHER, THE COLDER

One might think that the top of a mountain would be warmer than the bottom, since it's nearer the sun. In fact, it's much colder—so cold that even at the equator, very high mountains such as Kilimanjaro, in Tanzania, always have snow and ice on their peaks.

There are several reasons for this. First, higher up in the atmosphere, the air is thinner, and can't hold as much heat. Second, the sun hits mountain slopes at an angle, instead of directly from above, so its heating power is less concentrated. Lastly, rocky, icy mountain tops reflect heat away, instead of absorbing it like soil and plants do.

RAIN CATCHERS

As air approaches a mountainside, it is forced upward. As it rises, the air gets colder, the water in it **condenses** to form clouds, and rain or snow falls. Because of this, mountains are often very rainy, especially on the side nearest the sea, where the arriving air is moist and many clouds form. Sometimes, clouds cannot get past a mountain range. They drop all their rain on one side, and a desert, called a rainshadow desert, forms on the other side.

This illustration shows how a mountain range can force clouds to form, and rain or snow to fall.

Air cools as it rises

Water vapor in the air condenses and forms clouds; water falls as rain

Moist air blows in from the sea

Ocean

Far side of the mountain receives very little rain and is called a rainshadow desert

COSTA RICA CLOUDFOREST

In Monteverde, Costa Rica, the mountain forests, called cloudforests, are continually shrouded in wet, misty clouds. The air is so damp that every surface is covered with mosses and air plants. Instead of sucking up water through roots, they soak it up from the air.

A cloudforest in Costa Rica.

WHY SO WINDY?

In lowland areas, trees, hills, and buildings slow wind down, but high up in the atmosphere, winds can move much faster. When they hit a high mountain, especially above the treeline, the winds blast it with full force. In addition, wind speeds up even more as it is channeled around and over mountain peaks.

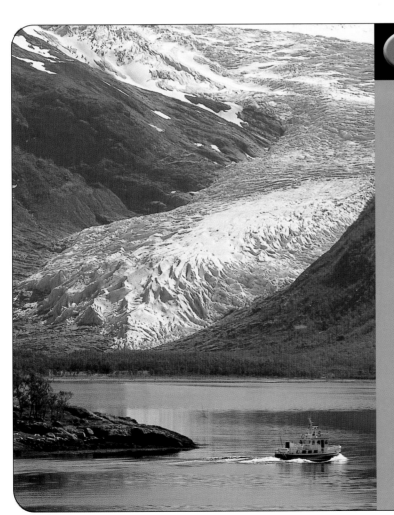

FACT FILE

MOUNTAIN WEATHER FACTS

• The average temperature on top of Mount Everest is about -17 °F (–27 °C). It can drop to -76 °F (–60 °C). At sea level, in nearby Dhaka, the average temperature is 77 °F (25 °C).

• Mount Washington, in New Hampshire, is one of the world's windiest peaks. The wind there averages 43 miles per hour (70 kph), and can gust to 229 miles per hour (370 kph).

• The heaviest snowfall ever measured in a single day hit mountains in Colorado in April 1921, when 74 inches (190 cm) of snow fell.

• If a lot of snow falls on a mountaintop, it can collect into ice and flow slowly down the mountain as a glacier.

This glacier in Norway has reached the foot of the mountains and is flowing into the sea.

DANGERS AND DISASTERS

Mountains can be deadly killers. The combination of steep slopes, sheer cliffs, thick forests, and bad weather makes it easy to get lost or injured. Because mountains are often remote and unpopulated, it's hard for people to get help if they run into trouble. Mountains can be dangerous to those living at the bottom of them. Thousands and thousands of people have lost their lives in volcanic eruptions, mudslides, and avalanches.

FEELING THE COLD

Cold is one of the biggest dangers facing mountaineers. Below a temperature of about 23 °F (−5 °C), body tissues can freeze, causing frostbite. Frostbite can damage noses, fingers, and toes so badly that they sometimes have to be cut off. Even more dangerous is hypothermia, which happens when the whole body gets too cold.

DANGEROUS DROPS

Mountains are full of places where it's easy to fall. As well as steep slopes, loose rocks, cliffs, and crags, high mountains have crevasses—deep cracks in glacier ice that can open up at any time. Mountaineers use special ladders to get across crevasses, but even the most experienced climbers sometimes fall into them.

AVALANCHE!

An avalanche happens when a mass of snow slips off a mountain. Avalanches can kill skiers and climbers caught in their path, and can even engulf whole villages. They are sometimes triggered by skiers disturbing the snow, but they can also happen by themselves.

LOCATION FILE

DEADLY EVEREST

More than 150 climbers have lost their lives climbing Mount Everest. The worst disaster happened on May 10, 1996, when several groups were trying to reach the summit at the same time. A sudden storm blew in, and eight people were killed trying to make their way back down to safety.

The famous British mountaineer Alison Hargreaves, pictured on Mount Everest in 1995. She died later that year during an ascent of another mountain, K2.

This car was caught in a mountain mudslide in Boulder Creek, California.

FACT FILE

MOUNTAIN DISASTERS

This table lists some of the deadliest mountain disasters in history.

DATE	PLACE	DISASTER
1883	Krakatoa, Indonesia	Volcanic eruption caused tsunamis that killed 36,000 people.
1902	Mt. Pelee, Martinique	30,000 were killed by being buried under volcanic ash.
1985	Ruiz, Colombia	Eruption melted ice, causing mudflows that killed 25,000 people.
1919	Kelut, Indonesia	Rock and mud flowing from the volcano claimed 5,000 lives.
1963	Alps, Italy	Vaiont Dam overflowed when the unstable hillside collapsed into the reservoir; 3,000 people died in floods.

ERUPTIONS AND MUDFLOWS

Scientists can predict some volcanic eruptions, but others still happen unexpectedly, causing major disasters. As well as flinging out rock, ash, and lava, volcanoes can cause massive mudflows, which often claim more lives than the eruption itself. This happens when a thick layer of ash coats a steep slope and is later saturated by heavy rain.

MOUNTAIN RESOURCES

What do people get from mountains? As well as being beautiful and providing fun for tourists (see page 38), mountains contain a range of natural resources, such as minerals, energy, and living things, that humans can collect and make use of.

MOUNTAIN MINERALS

Most mountains are made by huge movements in Earth's crust. As well as pushing rock up to form mountains, these forces squeeze rocks or heat them up, forming valuable minerals such as emeralds, and rocks such as marble. The upheaval of Earth's crust in mountain areas brings deposits of gold and other minerals nearer to Earth's surface, so mountains are a great place to find precious stones and metals. People also collect huge amounts of other rock, such as granite, sandstone, and limestone, from mountains to use in building.

DOWNHILL POWER

Mountains can make electricity, too. When water flows down mountains in rivers, it holds a store of energy. This energy can be converted into electricity by building dams and using the flow of water to turn turbines. This is called **hydroelectric power**, or HEP, and it is used a lot in mountainous countries such as Canada, Zaire, and Norway. More than 90 percent of Norway's energy comes from HEP.

A hydroelectric dam and power plant on the Kootenay River, in the Canadian Rocky Mountains.

Chinchillas come from the Andes Mountains in northern Chile. Their fur is among the thickest and softest in the world. Each of a chinchilla's hair follicles has up to 60 hairs growing from it, instead of one, as in most furry animals.

ANIMAL PRODUCTS

Because it is so thick and warm, hair or wool from mountain animals is often used to make luxury fabrics for humans to wear. For example, cashmere and pashmina wool come from Asian species of mountain goats. For a long time, humans have trapped other mountain animals, such as chinchillas and snow leopards, for their skins and fur. Many of these species are now protected by law to try to stop them from becoming extinct (see page 44).

FACT FILE

MOUNTAIN MATERIALS

Some of these items, which may have come from mountain areas, may be found in people's homes or neighborhoods.

- PUMICE STONE Used for rubbing off dead skin, pumice stone is made of cooled, hardened lava from volcanoes.
- EMERALDS Emeralds are green gemstones that are often found in mountain areas.
- ALUMINUM FOIL Made from bauxite, a mineral mined from mountains in Jamaica and Brazil.
- MARBLE This mountain rock is used to make countertops and statues. It comes in many colors, including pink, gray, black, and white.

MOUNTAIN PEOPLE

Mountains are among the harshest, most remote places on Earth—yet some people manage to survive and make a living there. They usually live in small, isolated villages that are very difficult to reach from the outside world. In the past, unable to trade or communicate with outsiders, some mountain communities were totally self-sufficient and developed their own unique languages and customs.

SHELTERED SPOTS

Most mountain settlements and homes are found in sheltered mountain valleys. There they are protected from the worst of the wind, and are close to a river or stream that can provide a water supply. Hardly anyone lives on the very top of a mountain; it is too windy and exposed. The highest villages in the world are in the Himalayas, at altitudes of around 18,040 feet (5,500 m)—not much more than half the height of Mount Everest.

Porters carrying luggage for mountain trekkers in Nepal.

BUILT FOR ALTITUDE

The higher up a mountain one goes, the less oxygen there is in the air. Above about 9,840 feet (3,000 m), the lack of oxygen makes many lowlanders feel ill. But people who live permanently in high mountains are adapted, or suited, to low-oxygen conditions. They tend to be short and stocky, which helps them to resist the cold. They have extra red blood cells for carrying oxygen around their bodies, and some even have extra-large lungs. Andean highlanders, for example, have lungs that are up to 25 percent bigger than a typical lowlander's lungs.

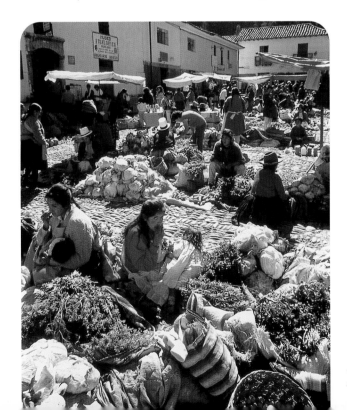

PEOPLE FILE

BABU CHHIRI

Babu Chhiri (far left) was one of the most famous of all Sherpa mountaineers, and was considered a national hero in Nepal. He climbed Everest 10 times in all, and in 2000, he set a world record for climbing the mountain in the fastest time—just under 17 hours (it normally takes days), although this record has since been broken. Tragically, he died on Everest in 2001, at the age of 35, from falling down a crevasse.

EARNING A LIVING

Despite the poor soil and harsh weather, many mountain dwellers are farmers. They grow mountain crops such as coffee, or herd tough mountain animals that can forage for their own food, such as yaks, llamas, or goats. Another source of work for mountain people is acting as guides and porters for tourists and climbers who visit the mountains. This is especially true in the Himalayas, where the Sherpa people are renowned for their climbing skills and knowledge of the mountains.

A market in an Andean mountain village in Peru.

FACT FILE

MOUNTAINOUS NATIONS

Here are some of the world's most mountainous countries:

• NEPAL Sandwiched between India and China, tiny Nepal borders the highest Himalayan peaks.
• BOLIVIA Around 60 percent of Bolivia's people live in the Andes mountains.
• ETHIOPIA The country is dominated by the huge fault mountains on either side of Africa's Great Rift Valley.
• IRAN Iran, in the Middle East, is a central plateau, surrounded by mountains.
• SWITZERLAND In the middle of the Alps, Switzerland is the most mountainous country in Europe.
• JAPAN Japan is 90 percent mountains.

MOUNTAIN TOWNS

Most mountain settlements are small towns or villages. Their buildings tend to be low and squat, so they don't get damaged by high winds. Big cities need good communication routes and plenty of flat land for building, so cities in the mountains are quite rare.

HIGH-ALTITUDE HOMES

Mountain houses are designed to deal with wind, cold, and heavy snow. They usually have small windows and big roofs that stick out a long way to stop snow from drifting up against the door. In parts of the Himalayas, traditional homes are built of mud bricks and have two stories. While the people live upstairs, the lower floor is used as a stable for farm animals, and the warmth from their bodies helps to heat the house. In the Alps, the snow itself is used to keep homes warm. Many houses have rocks or small fences fixed to their roofs to keep the snow from sliding off. It acts as a layer of roof insulation, trapping heat inside the house.

FACT FILE

CITIES ON TOP OF THE WORLD
The following are some of the highest cities in the world:
• Wenquan, China, is officially the world's highest city, at 16,728 feet (5,100 m).
• La Paz, Bolivia, at 11,906 feet (3,630 m), is the world's highest capital city.
• Potosi, another city in Bolivia, is even higher—13,415 feet (4,090 m).
• Leadville, Colorado, the highest city in the U.S., has an altitude of 10,201 feet (3,110 m).
• Lhasa, a city in Tibet, now ruled by China, is at 12,136 feet (3,700 m).

MOUNTAIN TRANSPORTATION

How does one reach a mountain town? Some mountain slopes are so steep that it's impossible to travel them straight up. Instead, mountain roads wind back and forth in a series of hairpin bends. This makes them less steep, but much longer. So even where there are roads, travel in the mountains can take a long time. On rough, steep tracks, animals are usually the best mode of transportation. Yaks, llamas, or mules can carry heavy loads, or even human passengers, safely up and down the steepest mountainsides.

Snow-covered wooden chalets (mountain cottages) in Valais, Switzerland.

The ruins of the ancient mountain city of Machu Picchu.

SAFE IN THE MOUNTAINS

In the past, castles and fortified towns were built on mountains to give them an advantage in case of an attack. In Greece, for example, people living in seaside towns often built another town in the nearest mountains that they could retreat to if invaders arrived.

LOCATION FILE

MACHU PICCHU

The ruined city of Machu Picchu is 7,872 feet (2,400 m) up in the Andes of Peru, South America. Built by the Inca people in the 15th century, it was probably an outpost of the Inca civilization. It lay deserted for more than 300 years, but since being rediscovered in 1911, it has become a major tourist attraction.

MOUNTAIN FARMS

Farming on a high mountain is no easy feat. The soil is easily blown or washed away down the steep hillsides, and farm animals have to contend with freezing weather. Yet mountain farms provide a living for millions of mountain farmers around the world. Many of them are subsistence farmers—they grow just enough food to keep themselves and their families alive.

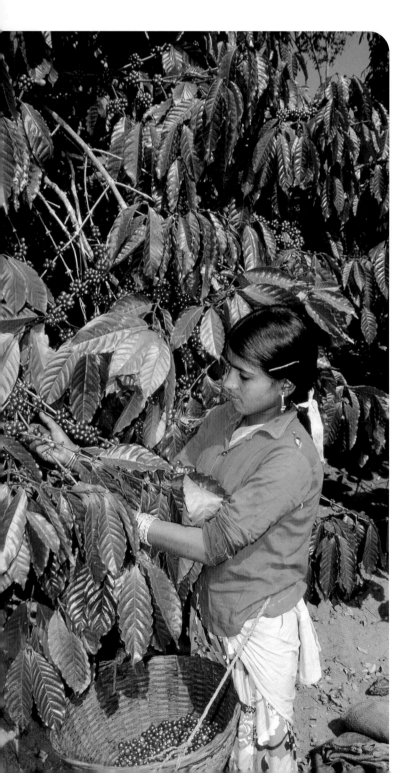

MOUNTAIN FARM ANIMALS

Mountain farm animals are bred from animals that live naturally at high altitudes, and so are used to the harsh conditions. In the Himalayas, farm yaks are related to the wild yaks that have lived there for millennia. Many mountain farmers also keep mountain sheep and goats. In the Andes, farmers breed alpacas and llamas for their wool, milk, and meat, and some also keep guinea pigs, which are native to the Andes mountains, to use as food.

MOUNTAIN CROPS

Mountain farmers grow hardy crops that can cope with thin soil and cold, windy weather, and provide a regular supply of food. The most popular include barley, quinoa (a type of cereal crop), and potatoes. A few crop plants, such as coffee and some types of berries, grow best at high altitude, as do medicinal herbs such as the Indian gentian. Some specialist mountain farmers grow crops such as these to sell.

A mountain farmer in India harvests coffee beans from a coffee bush. Most types of coffee grow best at high altitudes.

YAK FACTS

For isolated mountain farmers, the best animals are those that have many different uses. The most useful of all is probably the yak. It provides:

• Milk, for drinking and making into butter. The butter is used as lamp fuel.

• Meat, which can be eaten fresh or preserved by drying.

• Leather, for making shoes and bags.

• Thick, wooly hair, for making rope, blankets, and clothes.

• Dung, which can be dried and used as fuel.

• Heat from its body, which can be used to heat homes.

• Transportation, for both people and goods.

These Mongolian farmers are milking their yaks at the summer grazing meadows.

TERRACES

Terraces are used on mountain farms around the world. They are steps dug into a hillside and supported with walls. This creates small areas of level land for farming, and stops soil and water from being washed away.

Bolivian farmers in the countryside around La Paz, in the Andes, harvesting potatoes.

UP AND DOWN

In the Swiss Alps, as in many mountain areas, farmers move their animals up the mountains in the spring and summer to feed on the fresh young grass. In the winter, the animals are moved back down to lower altitudes to keep warm.

MOUNTAIN INDUSTRIES

In some parts of the world, mountains are home to huge industrial activity, especially mining the valuable stones and metals that mountains contain. Industries provide mountain people with jobs, but they can also scar mountains forever.

MOUNTAIN MINING

Mining is a huge mountain industry. It ranges from small-scale methods, such as **panning** for gold, which do not affect the landscape, to massive open-cast mining and quarrying operations. These large operations involve bulldozing or blasting the mountainside open to gain access to the precious deposits. Some mountains have been changed forever by mining. At Potosi, in Bolivia, for example, Cerro Rico (Rich Hill) has been mined so extensively for silver that the mountain is 984 feet (300 m) shorter than it used to be.

Local people search through leftover rubble and dust outside an emerald mine in Colombia, hoping to find valuable emerald scraps.

LOCATION FILE

THE MUZO MINE

The Andean town of Muzo, Colombia, is home to the world's biggest emerald mine. Besides the hundreds of miners who are officially employed at the mine, thousands of local people make a living by picking through the leftover dirt for emerald fragments. These emerald-hunters are known as Guaqueros.

COTTAGE INDUSTRIES

A cottage industry is an industry that's carried out on a small scale at home, instead of by mass production in big factories. In mountain areas, where it's hard to build factories, cottage industries are very important. The most common are weaving and making clothes and leather goods, using the hair and skin of mountain farm animals such as sheep, yaks, and goats. In the Atlas Mountains of North Africa, for example, women weave sheep's wool and goat hair into rugs that can be sold to tourists.

MOUNTAIN LOGGING

Logging—cutting down trees for their wood—happens wherever there are trees. It's more common in lowland areas where the wood is easily taken away, but as lowland forests get used up, loggers in some areas have moved to mountain forests instead. Logging can cause problems on hillsides, as it leads to soil being washed away (see page 42).

Moroccan mountain weavers and rug-makers come to this market in the city of Marrakesh to sell their wares.

PEOPLE FILE

JAMES MARSHALL

In 1848, carpenter James Marshall was building a sawmill on the American River, in Coloma, California, when he found tiny grains of gold in the river water. Although he tried to keep it a secret, his discovery led to one of the biggest gold mining operations in history—the California Gold Rush. Millions of people flocked to the Californian mountains, and millions of dollars' worth of gold was extracted. John Marshall, however, never struck lucky again, and died in poverty.

MOUNTAIN TOURISM

Mountains attract millions of tourists every year. Their wild landscapes offer a chance to escape from busy cities and developed areas, and act as a playground for dozens of different sports and activities.

AMAZING VIEWS

People like to climb mountains for the challenge, but also for the view or to see amazing sights, such as a moving glacier or the crater of an active volcano. In Hawaii, for example, the Volcanoes National Park, where tourists can see lava flowing from Kilauea, the world's most active volcano, is the most popular tourist attraction in the state.

EXCITING SPORTS

Steep slopes, snow, and wide, open spaces mean mountains are the perfect place for exciting sports. The most popular mountain sport is skiing. Around the world, ski resorts attract millions of tourists and employ millions of people every year. Other mountain sports include walking, climbing, snowboarding, white-water rafting, and mountain biking, as well as several more extreme sports.

JOBS IN TOURISM

While it can be hard to find normal office jobs in mountain areas, tourism creates huge numbers of jobs doing things like teaching people to ski and rock-climb, leading guided walks, and working in hotels. A lot of these jobs are casual work and seasonal, but they still provide many people with income. In countries such as Canada, Switzerland, Nepal, and Scotland, mountain tourism makes up an important part of the economy.

Tourists watch lava from a Hawaiian volcano flowing into the sea.

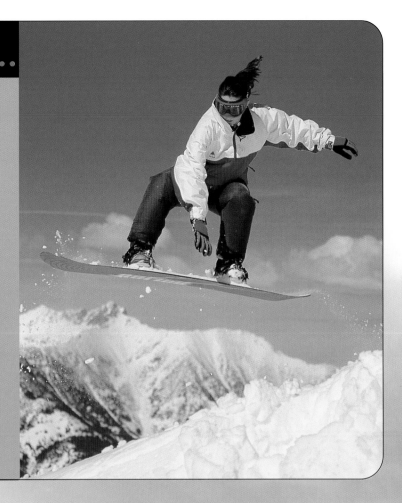

EXTREME SPORTS

Here are just a few of the more extreme and unusual mountain sports:

• CANYONING Wading, rappelling, and swimming down the canyons and waterfalls of a mountain river.

• ZORBING or SPHEREING Rolling down a steep slope inside a giant inflatable plastic sphere.

• PARAGLIDING Jumping off high places using a parachute-like device to fly back to the valley floor.

• ICE CLIMBING Climbing up glaciers or frozen waterfalls.

• ZIPLINING Sliding along a cable strung between two high points.

Snowboarding (above) and skiing are the most popular mountain sports.

LOCATION FILE

ASPEN, COLORADO

In the 1930s, Aspen, a run-down former mining town in the Rocky Mountains, had a population of just 700. Then, in 1935, people started developing it for skiing. Today, it is one of the best-known ski resorts in the world and is famous for its celebrity visitors. It has a permanent population of 7,000, which swells to more than 40,000 during peak season, and is one of the wealthiest towns in the U.S.

MANAGING MOUNTAINS

Mountain areas can easily be damaged by too much industry, farming, or tourism. Managing mountains means controlling the way mountain areas are developed, to try to preserve them and keep them clean.

MOUNTAIN DEVELOPMENT

Many people want to go to the mountains on vacation, to take part in skiing and other sports, and to experience the natural beauty of a wilderness area. Many people also want to develop mountain areas in order to create jobs for local people. However, by building hotels, roads, ski-lifts, public toilets, and so on, people are in danger of destroying the very untamed beauty that makes mountains attractive. So it is important to manage mountain development to preserve a balance between keeping wild areas wild, and making it possible to visit and enjoy them.

NATIONAL PARKS

A national park is an area of land that is set aside to protect it from damage and overdevelopment. Many mountain regions have been made into national parks to preserve them for the future. A typical national park has visitor facilities such as toilets, garbage cans, and marked trails, allowing people to visit a wild area while keeping environmental damage and pollution to a minimum. There may also be park wardens who patrol the park and protect wildlife.

WHO OWNS MOUNTAINS?

Unlike lowland areas, mountains are usually not bought and sold as land. This is partly because they make poor farmland and are hard to build on. Instead, mountain areas are often owned by the governments of the countries they lie in, and it is up to these governments to make laws to keep mountains safe and protect their wildlife and landscapes.

LOCATION FILE

YELLOWSTONE

Yellowstone National Park, in the northwestern U.S., is the oldest national park in the world. It was founded in 1872 and has nearly three million visitors a year. It covers nearly 2.5 million acres (1 million ha) of mountainous territory and is home to mountain animals such as wolves, bighorn sheep, and grizzly bears.

A park ranger at Yellowstone uses special equipment to check levels of air pollution in the park.

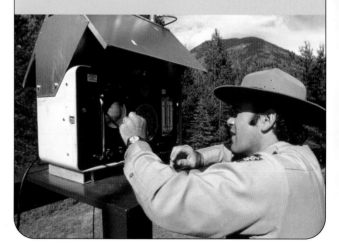

However, in many countries, especially those with ongoing civil wars, such as Colombia and Afghanistan, mountain areas may be ruled by local clans or rebel groups. This makes it hard for governments to control mountain areas.

SCOTLAND'S CAIRNGORMS

The Cairngorm Mountains, in Scotland, are an example of a mountain area that was caught in a clash of conflicting interests. While developers wanted to build more and more ski resorts and hotels to make money, environmentalists wanted to keep tourists out of some areas in case they disturbed rare mountain birds such as the golden eagle, snow bunting, and capercaillie. To try to end this conflict, the Cairngorms were made into a national park in 2003.

A golden eagle, one of the rare mountain bird species that campaigners in the Cairngorms have fought to protect.

MOUNTAINS IN DANGER

Mountains might seem tough, but in fact, mountain ecosystems are fragile and easily damaged, and many mountain areas are threatened by pollution and mismanagement.

STEEP SLOPES

One reason that mountains are so vulnerable is their steep slopes. The soil there is held in place by trees and plants. Methods such as terracing (see page 35) can keep soil from being washed away, but if a hillside is deforested (stripped of its trees) and then left bare, the soil can disappear within a few decades. This can harm whole mountain food webs, as animals depend on soil and plants for their food. It can also harm humans, as the steady washing away of soil over a long period pollutes rivers and depletes farmland. Sometimes loose rocks and soil may crash down the mountain in a landslide, flattening towns or blocking rivers and roads.

POLLUTION FROM FAR AWAY

Even mountains that are far away from towns and cities can be seriously affected by pollution. Chemical waste from cars and factories rises up into the atmosphere and makes rainwater acidic. Because clouds are especially likely to drop their rain on mountains (see page 24), mountain areas get the worst of this acid rain. It can damage forests and change the chemical balance of mountain lakes, killing the wildlife that lives there. On top of this, visitors to mountains can cause a pollution problem by leaving litter behind.

An aerial view of mountain forests in the state of Washington. On the right, the forests have been cut down, leaving bare hillside and destroying the habitat of mountain forest animals.

MESSY MOUNT EVEREST

Since it was first climbed in 1953 by Sir Edmund Hillary and Tenzing Norgay, Mount Everest has become a dumping ground. Hundreds of people have climbed to the top, and the route is now littered with plastic waste and used oxygen canisters. There are even dozens of frozen dead bodies. Since the year 2000, several climbing expeditions have gone up the mountain just to clean up some of the litter.

Waste left on Mount Everest.

WILDLIFE IN DANGER

Mountain plants and animals are specially adapted for living in their high-altitude homes. If their habitats are damaged—for example, if a mountain forest is chopped down for wood, or to make room for a ski slope—they have nowhere else to go and are in danger of dying out. Some mountain animals are also at risk from poachers who hunt them for their fur, horns, or meat.

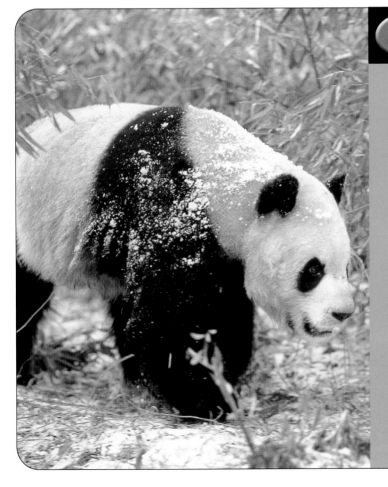

FACT FILE

ENDANGERED MOUNTAIN ANIMALS

Many mountain animals are endangered (at risk of dying out). Here are just a few of them:
• Snow leopards in the Himalayas are at risk from poachers and habitat loss.
• Mountain gorillas in central Africa are hunted for meat, and are also killed in wars and by viruses.
• Giant pandas in China are dying out because of deforestation of the mountain bamboo forests where they live.
• Kakapos—flightless parrots that live in mountain forests in New Zealand—have declined since humans took cats, dogs, and other hunting animals there.
• Grizzly bears in the U.S. are endangered because so many have been killed to protect humans and livestock.

A rare giant panda in the wild.

CONSERVING MOUNTAINS

Today, although some mountain areas and plant and animal species are still in danger, governments and organizations around the world are making efforts to conserve (save) them.

PARKS AND RESERVES

National parks help to conserve mountains by keeping them safe from crimes (such as poaching, pollution, and stealing eggs) and overdevelopment. Park rangers and wardens guard against poaching and control the numbers of tourists entering the park. Some countries also have special wildlife reserves, where one or more species of endangered animals can live in safety. However, managing mountain areas in this way is very expensive, and some poorer countries cannot afford to do it.

CONSERVATION LAWS

Governments can help to conserve mountains and other wild areas using laws. For example, hunting endangered wild animals such as snow leopards is now illegal in most countries. There are also laws that force developers to obtain planning permission before they can develop a mountain area into a tourist resort. If the development would damage the landscape or wildlife too much, permission can be denied. However, like all laws, these laws have to be enforced—and in remote mountain regions, that can be very difficult.

In Sweden, many forests are now sustainable, which means each tree that is cut down for timber is replaced.

RULES FOR VISITORS

Many national parks have rules for their visitors to protect the local landscape and wildlife. For example, asking tourists to stick to specially built paths can make sure other parts of the mountain aren't eroded away by thousands of feet. Most parks also ask tourists not to start fires, leave litter, or collect plants. At some times of the year, certain areas of a national park may be closed to the public so that animals can be left alone to breed and raise their babies safely.

A Nubian ibex with her calf.

GLOSSARY

Active An active volcano is one that erupts regularly.

Adapt When a plant or animal species adapts, it changes over time to suit its habitat.

Altitude Height above sea level.

Condenses Changes from a gas (such as water vapor) into a liquid.

Deciduous Deciduous trees and shrubs shed their leaves in the winter.

Dormant A dormant volcano has stopped erupting, but could erupt again one day.

Ecosystem A habitat and all the plants and animals that live in it.

Erosion Wearing away of rock and soil.

Evergreen Evergreen trees and shrubs keep their leaves year-round.

Extinct If a plant or animal species is extinct, it has died out forever. An extinct volcano is one that will never erupt again.

GIS (Geographic Information System) Computer technology used for making and displaying maps.

Glaciers Rivers of ice that inch slowly down a mountain, fed by the snow and ice that collects on top, or a sheet of ice covering a large area.

GPS (Global Positioning System) Technology that works out the positions of points on the globe using satellites.

Habitats Places where a plant or animal species lives, such as a forest or a mountain meadow.

HEP (Hydroelectric power) Power generated by harnessing the energy of water flowing downhill.

Landforms The different shapes land is formed into, such as mountains and valleys.

Magma Hot, molten rock inside Earth.

Niche The unique role a plant or animal species has in its ecosystem.

Orogenesis A scientific name for what happens when mountains are formed.

Panning Trying to find gold by swirling rocks and mud from a river around in a pan. If there is any gold, it sinks to the bottom.

Remote sensing Recording information about Earth from far away, usually by using satellites.

Satellites Machines sent up into space to orbit (move around) Earth. Some satellites are used to take photos of Earth or record other geographical information.

Seamounts Mountains under the sea.

Strata Layers found in rock.

Symbiosis When two plant or animal species live together in a way that helps both partners.

Tectonic plates The massive sections of rock that make up Earth's crust.

Terrain A type of land with particular features. For example, mountain terrain can be very rocky and steep.

Tsunamis Massive waves caused by movements in Earth below the ocean floor, such as earthquakes or volcanic eruptions. Tsunamis can travel long distances across oceans before crashing onto the shore, where they often cause serious damage.

FURTHER INFORMATION

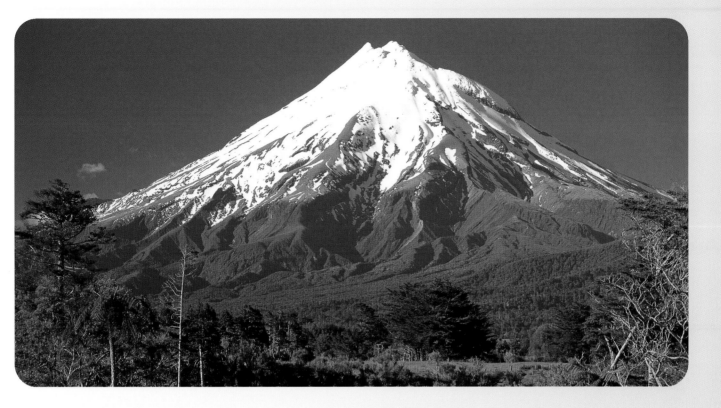

WEB SITES TO VISIT

http://www.mountain.org/education/

This site is intended as a fun guide to mountains. It has links to other sites where you can see videos of mountain animals and listen to mountain musical instruments.

The Mountain Institute

1828 L Street NW, Suite 725

Washington, D.C. 20036

Tel: (202) 452-1636

E-mail: summit@mountain.org

http://www.enchantedlearning.com/subjects/volcano/activities.shtml

A set of information pages, activities, and volcano experiments to try.

Enchanted Learning

P.O. Box 321

Mercer Island, WA 98040-0321

Tel: (206) 232-4880

E-mail: info@EnchantedLearning.com

http://www.nps.gov/yell/home.htm

The official Web site of Yellowstone National Park, with pages of information on wildlife and geological features, plus games and activities.

Yellowstone National Park

P.O. Box 168

WY 82190-0168

Tel: (307) 344-7381

E-mail: yell_visitor_services@nps.gov

BOOKS TO READ

Chambers, Catherine. *Mountains*. Chicago: Heinemann Library, 2000.

Harris, Tim. *Mountains and Highlands.* Austin, Tex.: Raintree Steck-Vaughn, 2003.

Taylor, David. *Endangered Mountain Animals.* New York: Crabtree Publishing Company, 1995.

Venables, Stephen. *To the Top: The Story of Mt. Everest.* Cambridge, Mass.: Candlewick Press, 2003.

INDEX